Little Mitchie

PLANET YUM

A SPACE EXPLORER'S COOKBOOK

CREATING YOUNG NONFICTION READERS

Little Mitchie books spark curiosity and support early nonfiction reading for students in Grades 2-3. Designed to build vocabulary, support second language learners, and prepare readers for middle-grade content, each book includes helpful tips for parents and educators to build confidence and deepen understanding of the world.

TIPS FOR READING NONFICTION WITH BEGINNING READERS

Talk about Nonfiction

Begin by explaining that nonfiction books give us information that is true. The book will be organized around a specific topic or idea, and we may learn new facts through reading.

Look at the Parts

Most nonfiction books have helpful features. Our *Little Mitchie* titles include color photographs and graphic aids, a table of contents, a glossary, and an index. Share the purpose of these features with your reader.

Color Photos and Graphic Aids

A lot of information can be found by "reading" photos, charts, maps, and other graphic aids found within nonfiction texts. Help your reader learn more about the different ways information can be displayed.

Table of Contents

Located at the front of the book, this list shows the big ideas within the text and the page numbers where they can be found.

Glossary

Located at the back of the book, the glossary defines key words and phrases that are related to the topic. These words and phrases can be found in the text in colored type.

Index

Located at the back of the book, an index is an alphabetical list of topics and the page numbers where they can be found.

With a little help and guidance about reading nonfiction, you can feel good about introducing a young reader to the world of *Little Mitchie* nonfiction books.

Little Mitchie is an imprint of:

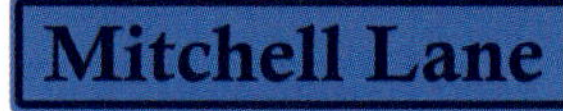

2001 SW 31st Avenue
Hallandale, FL 33009
mitchelllanepub.com

First Edition, 2027.

Author: Joanne Mattern
Designer: Bobbie Houser
Editor: Madison Greve

Library of Congress Cataloging-in-Publication Data
Title: Planet Yum: A Space Explorer's Cookbook / by Joanne Mattern

Description: Hallandale, FL : Mitchell Lane Publishers, [2027]

Identifiers:
ISBN 979-8-89260-929-6 (library bound)
ISBN 979-8-90145-015-4 (eBook)

Library of Congress Control Number: 2026936388

PHOTO CREDITS
Alamy: Marius Hainal, 7; Cavan Images, 11; Shutterstock: kuvona, cover, 1, 15; Taras Grebinets, 4; Viktoriia Ablohina, 5; yar-andy, 9; John_Walker_Shutter, 13; Bettina Calder, 17; Ezume Images, 19; MBLifestyle, 21.

TABLE OF CONTENTS

HOW TO USE THIS BOOK

The kitchen is a great place to have fun! This book will help you make some delicious recipes.

Read each recipe first. Be sure to have everything you need in place before you start. Check that no one is **allergic** to any of the ingredients.

Wash your hands before you start.

Have an adult close by. Let them use knives and the stove.

Now, get ready to cook up some fun!

CONVERSION CHART

1 gallon =
4 quarts
8 pints
16 cups
128 ounces

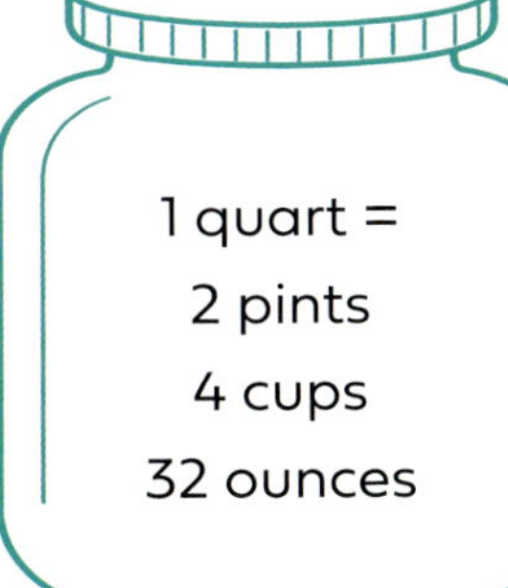

1 cup =
16 tablespoons
8 ounces

¾ cup =
12 tablespoons
6 ounces

½ cup =
8 tablespoons
4 ounces

⅓ cup =
5⅓ tablespoons
2⅔ ounces

¼ cup =
4 tablespoons
2 ounces

3 teaspoons = 1 tablespoon (½ ounce)
2 tablespoons = ⅛ cup (1 ounce)
4 tablespoons = ¼ cup (2 ounces)
5⅓ tablespoons = ⅓ cup (2⅔ ounces)
8 tablespoons = ½ cup (4 ounces)
12 tablespoons = ¾ cup (6 ounces)
32 tablespoons = 2 cups (16 ounces)

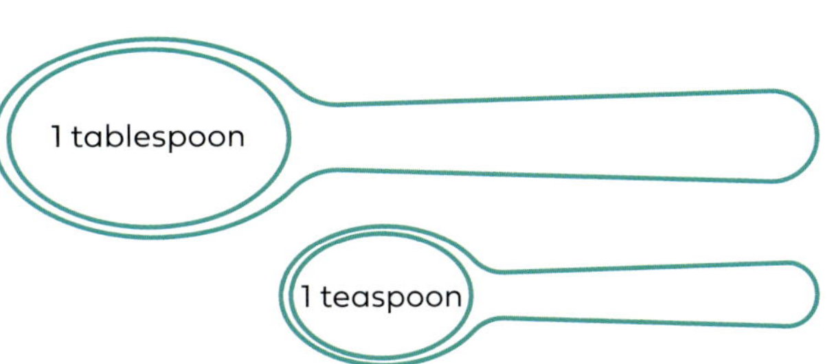

Chapter 1

ROCKET FRUIT SKEWERS

"What did you learn in school today, Kira?" her older sister, Callie, asked.

"We learned about outer space," Kira said. "Our teacher showed a video about rocket ships. Then we made some rockets out of fruit. It was fun and healthy. I want to make some for us at home."

“All right,” Callie said. “I’ll help you. Let’s blast off to the kitchen!”

You will need:

1 banana

4 strawberries

4 **kiwis**

4 wooden **skewers**

Directions:

Peel the banana and ask an adult to cut off the ends. Then cut the rest of the banana into 8 pieces.

Wash the strawberries and ask an adult to cut off the leaves. Then cut each strawberry in half across the middle so the tops have round tips and the bottoms are flat.

Ask an adult to peel the skin off of the kiwis and cut the fruit so that each piece is approximately the size of a strawberry half.

Slide the fruit onto a skewer in this order: banana, kiwi, strawberry. Use only the bottom parts of the strawberries for this step.

Repeat this pattern until you have almost filled the skewers with fruit. Finish with a strawberry top pointing out to make the tops of your rocket ships.

FUN FOOD FACT!
Bananas grow in large bunches called hands. Each banana is a finger!

Chapter 2

YOGURT PRETZEL ALIENS

"What a great movie!" Thomas exclaimed. "My favorite part was when the **aliens** learned how to ride bikes! That was really funny."

"It would be fun to play with an alien," his friend Charles said.

“We can make some aliens you can play with and eat,” Thomas’s mother said. “Come in the kitchen and help me make aliens out of pretzels.”

“That sounds fun!” the boys said. They ran into the kitchen.

You will need:

1 bag of yogurt-covered pretzels

1 package of candy eyes

White cookie icing

Directions:

Place a sheet of wax paper on a tray.

Lay the pretzels on the sheet.

Squeeze icing into the 2 holes at the top of each pretzel. The bottom holes will be the mouths.

Press a candy eye into the middle of each dot of icing.

Put the tray of pretzels in the refrigerator for 1–2 hours or until the icing gets hard.

FUN FOOD FACT!
Yogurt has been around for more than 7,000 years.

Chapter 3

BLAST-OFF BREAKFAST

"What's for breakfast?" Jordan asked.

"We're going on a rocket ship this morning," his father said. He pointed to the plate on the table. "Are you ready to blast off for Planet Breakfast?"

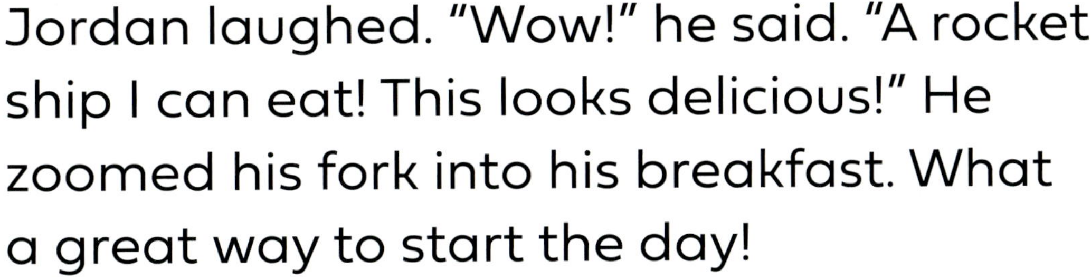

Jordan laughed. “Wow!” he said. “A rocket ship I can eat! This looks delicious!” He zoomed his fork into his breakfast. What a great way to start the day!

You will need:

1 egg

1 slice of butter

1 teaspoon of water

1 slice of bread

1 slice of deli meat

Directions:

Crack the egg into a bowl with a little bit of water and stir well. Ask an adult to melt the butter in the pan, add the egg mixture, and stir until **scrambled**.

Ask an adult to cut the bread into 3 small triangles and 1 rectangle. Lay down a piece of deli meat and place the bread pieces on top of it.

Set 1 triangle above the short end of the rectangle, pointing out like the top of a rocket ship. Then place 1 triangle on each side of the bottom end to make the rocket's **fins**.

Ask an adult to cut the meat along the edges of the rocket ship and throw away the scraps.

Move the bread to a plate, remake the shape of the rocket ship, and lay the meat on top.

Place the scrambled egg on the bottom of the plate to look like the rocket is blasting off.

FUN FOOD FACT!

Ostriches lay the largest eggs of any bird. An ostrich egg can weigh approximately 3 pounds.

Chapter 4

Pizza Planets

"Hooray! It's pizza night!" Fran said as she joined her family in the kitchen. Every Friday night, the family had pizza.

"It is," said her brother, Randy. "But tonight, we are doing something different."

"No pizza?" Fran asked.

"Oh, yes," her mother replied. "Tonight, we are making our own pizza planets!"

"How can we do that?" Fran asked.

Fran's mother pointed to the food on the counter. "Use your imagination," she said. "Then we will take off for the pizza planet!"

You will need:

4 English muffins

1 jar of pizza sauce

1 jar of black olives

1 green or red bell pepper

8 slices of mozzarella cheese

Directions:

Ask an adult to slice the English muffins in half.

Top each muffin half with pizza sauce.

Ask an adult to chop the pepper and olives into tiny pieces.

Add the chopped pepper and olives to each pizza to make the surface of your planet.

Ask an adult to place the pizzas on a tray and toast them in the oven until the cheese melts.

FUN FOOD FACT!
Pizza was first made in Italy approximately 200 years ago.

GLOSSARY

aliens (ALE-ee-enz)—creatures from other planets

allergic (uh-LER-jik)—having a bad reaction to a food

fins (FINZ)—flat pieces added to the bottoms of rocket ships to help with steering

kiwis (KEE-weez)—small, round, green fruits with brown fuzzy skin

ostriches (AWS-trich-iz)—large African birds with long necks

scrambled (SKRAM-buhld)—to cook eggs while beating and stirring them

skewers (SKYOO-erz)—long, thin sticks used to hold food

FURTHER READING

Highlights for Children. *Ultimate Science Cookbook for Kids.* Highlights Press, 2025.

Kartes, Danielle. *The Best Kids Cookbook.* Tommy Nelson, 2025.

ON THE INTERNET

Mifsud, Anne. "10 Space Themed Snacks Your Kids Will Love." Easy Kids Parties.com.
https://easykidsparties.com/space-themed-snacks/
You'll find fun and tasty space-themed recipe ideas in this easy-to-follow article.

"Space Themed Treats for Kids." Jordan's Easy Entertaining.com.
https://jordanseasyentertaining.com/space-themed-food-for-kids/
This article has many different space-themed recipes for kids and adults to try.

INDEX

ABOUT THE AUTHOR

Joanne Mattern loves snacking and eating fun food! She has written many nonfiction books for children, including cookbooks and books about holidays. Joanne lives in New York State with her family.